FARM BALLADS

BY

WILL CARLETON

NEW YORK AND LONDON

HARPER & BROTHERS PUBLISHERS

TO

MY MOTHER

PREFACE

THESE poems have been written under various, and in some cases difficult, conditions: in the open air, "with team afield"; in the student's den, with the ghosts of unfinished lessons hovering gloomily about; amid the rush and roar of railroad travel, which trains of thought are not prone to follow; and in the editor's sanctum, where the dainty feet of the Muses do not always deign to tread.

The author has been asked, by friends in all parts of the country, to put his poems into a more durable form than they have hitherto possessed; and it is in accordance with these requests that he now presents "Farm Ballads" to the public.

1873

PREFACE TO REVISED EDITION

IT has been deemed best to revise and enlarge this book, bringing it up in size to other members of the " FARM SERIES."

The additional numbers are of two classes : poems written some ten years ago, and omitted in former editions, and those written during the past year. The author has not taken pains to distinguish these from each other by inserting dates ; he prefers to let each one stand upon its own merits, or stumble against its own demerits, without the advantage or disadvantage of a published birth-year.

He is sorry the whole work is not better, and still rejoices that the public have shown a continuous appetite for the book. He thanks them, and takes courage for future work.

1882.

CONTENTS

FARM BALLADS

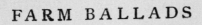

FARM BALLADS

FARM BALLADS

BETSEY AND I ARE OUT

DRAW up the papers, lawyer, and make 'em good and
    stout;
Things at home are crossways, and Betsey and I are
    out.
We, who have worked together so long as man and
    wife,
Must pull in single harness the rest of our nat'ral life.

"What is the matter?" say you.   I swan it's hard to
    tell!
Most of the years behind us we've passed by very
    well;
I have no other woman, she has no other man—
Only we've lived together as long as we ever can.

So I have talked with Betsey, and Betsey has talked
    with me,
So we've agreed together that we can't never agree;

Not that we've catched each other in any terrible
    crime;
We've been a-gathering this for years, a little at a time.

There was a stock of temper we both had for a start,
Though we never suspected 'twould take us two apart;
I had my various failings, bred in the flesh and bone;
And Betsey, like all good women, had a temper of
    her own.

First thing I remember whereon we disagreed
Was something concerning heaven—a difference in our
    creed;
We arg'ed the thing at breakfast, we arg'ed the thing
    at tea,
And the more we arg'ed the question the more we
    didn't agree.

And the next that I remember was when we lost a cow;
She had kicked the bucket for certain, the question
    was only—How?
I held my own opinion, and Betsey another had;
And when we were done a-talkin', we both of us was
    mad.

And the next that I remember, it started in a joke;
But full for a week it lasted, and neither of us spoke.
And the next was when I scolded because she broke
    a bowl;
And she said I was mean and stingy, and hadn't any
    soul.

And so that bowl kept pourin' dissensions in our cup;
And so that blamed old cow was always a-comin' up;
And so that heaven we arg'ed no nearer to us got,
But it gave us a taste of somethin' a thousand times
    as hot.

And so the thing kept workin', and all the self-same
    way :
Always somethin' to arg'e, and somethin' sharp to say;
And down on us came the neighbors, a couple dozen
    strong,
And lent their kindest sarvice for to help the thing
    along.

And there has been days together—and many a weary
    week—
We was both of us cross and crabbed, and both too
    proud to speak ;
And I have been thinkin' and thinkin', the whole of
    the winter and fall,
If I can't live kind with a woman, why, then, I won't
    at all.

And so I have talked with Betsey, and Betsey has
    talked with me,
And we have agreed together that we can't never
    agree ;
And what is hers shall be hers, and what is mine
    shall be mine ;
And I'll put it in the agreement, and take it to her
    to sign.

Write on the paper, lawyer—the very first paragraph—
Of all the farm and live-stock that she shall have her
    half;
For she has helped to earn it, through many a weary
    day:
And it's nothing more than justice that Betsey has
    her pay.

Give her the house and homestead: a man can thrive
    and roam,
But women are skeery critters, unless they have a
    home;
And I have always determined, and never failed to
    say,
That my wife never should want a home if I was taken
    away.

There is a little hard cash that's drawin' tol'rable
    pay:
Just a few thousand dollars laid by for a rainy day;
Safe in the hands of good men, and easy to get at;
Put in another clause there, and give her half of
    that.

Yes, I see you smile, Sir, at my givin' her so much;
Yes, divorces is cheap, Sir, but I take no stock in
    such!
True and fair I married her, when she was blithe and
    young;
And Betsey was al'ays good to me—exceptin' with her
    tongue.

Once, when I was young as you, and not so smart,
    perhaps,
For me she mittened a lawyer, and several other
    chaps;
And all of them fellers was flustered, and fairly taken
    down,
And I for a time was counted the luckiest man in
    town.

Once when I had a fever—I won't forget it soon--
I was hot as a basted turkey and crazy as a loon!
Never an hour went by me when she was out of
    sight—
She nursed me true and tender, and stuck to me day
    and night.

And if ever a house was tidy, and ever a kitchen
    clean,
Her house and kitchen was tidy as any I ever seen;
And I don't complain of Betsey, or any of her acts,
Exceptin' as when we've quarrelled, and twitted each
    other on facts.

So draw up the papers, lawyer: and I'll go home to-
    night.
And read the agreement to her, and see if it's all
    right;
And then, in the mornin', I'll sell to a tradin' man I
    know,
And kiss the child that was left to us, and out in the
    world I'll go.

And one thing put in the paper, that first to me
   didn't occur:
That when I am dead at last she bring me back to
   her;
And lay me under the maples I planted years ago,
When she and I was happy; before we quarrelled so.

And when she dies I wish that she would be laid by
   me;
And, lyin' together in silence, perhaps we might agree;
And if ever we meet in heaven, I wouldn't think it
   queer
If we loved each other the better for what we quarrelled here.

HOW BETSEY AND I MADE UP

GIVE us your hand, Mr. Lawyer: how do you do to-
    day?
You drew up that paper — I s'pose you want your
    pay.
Don't cut down your figures; make it an X or a V;
For that 'ere written agreement was just the makin'
    of me!

Goin' home that evenin' I tell you I was blue,
Thinkin' of all my troubles, and what I was goin'
    to do;
And if my hosses hadn't been the steadiest team
    alive,
They'd 've tipped me over for certain; for I couldn't
    see where to drive.

No—for I was laborin' under a heavy load;
No—for I was travellin' an entirely different road;
For I was a-tracin' over the path of our lives ag'in,
And observin' where we missed the way, and where
    we might have been.

And many a corner we'd turned that just to a quarrel
    led,
When I ought to 've held my temper, and driven
    straight ahead;
And the more I thought it over the more these mem-
    ories came,
And the more I struck the opinion that I was the
    most to blame.

And things I had long forgotten kept risin' in my
    mind,
Of little matters betwixt us, where Betsey was good
    and kind;
And these things flashed all through me, as you know
    things sometimes will
When a feller's alone in the darkness, and everything
    is still.

"But," says I, "we're too far along to take another
    track,
And when I put my hand to the plough I do not oft
    turn back;
And 'tain't an uncommon thing now for couples to
    smash in two;"
And so I set my teeth together, and vowed I'd see it
    through.

And when I come in sight o' the house 'twas some'at
    in the night,
And just as I turned a hill-top I see the kitchen
    light;

Which often a han'some pictur' to a hungry person
    makes,
But it don't interest a man so much that's goin' to
    pull up stakes.

And when I went in the house, the table was set for
    me—
As good a supper 's ever I saw, or ever want to
    see;
And I crammed the agreement down in my pocket as
    well as ever I could,
And fell to eatin' my victuals, which somehow didn't
    taste good.

And Betsey, she pretended to be lookin' all round the
    house;
But she watched my side coat-pocket like a cat would
    watch a mouse;
And then she went to foolin' a little with her
    cup,
And intently readin' a newspaper—a-holdin' it wrong
    side up.

And when I'd done with my supper, I drawed the
    agreement out,
And give it to her without a word, for she knowed
    what 'twas about;
And then I hummed a little tune; but now and then
    a note
Got bu'sted by some animal that hopped up in my
    throat.

Then Betsey she went an' took her specs from off the
    mantel-shelf,
And read the agreement over quite softly to herself;
Read it by little and little; for her eyes is gettin' old,
And lawyers' writin' ain't no print, especially when it's
    cold.

And after she'd read a little she give my arm a touch,
And kindly said she was afraid I was 'lowin' her too
    much;
But when she was through she went for me, her face
    a-streamin' with tears,
And kissed me for the first time in half-a-dozen years!

I don't know what you'll think, Sir—I didn't come to
    inquire—
But I picked up that agreement and stuffed it in the
    fire;
And I told her we'd bury the hatchet alongside of the
    cow;
And we struck an agreement never to have another
    row.

And I told her in the future I wouldn't speak cross
    nor rash
If half the crockery in the house was broken all to
    smash;
And she said, in regards to heaven, we'd try and prove
    its worth
By startin' a branch establishment, and runnin' it here
    on earth.

And so we sat a-talkin' three-quarters of the night,
And opened our hearts to each other until they both
    grew light;
And the days when I was winnin' her away from so
    many men
Was nothin' to that evenin' I courted her over again.

Next mornin' an ancient virgin took pains to call on
    us,
Her lamp all trimmed and a-burnin' — to kindle an-
    other fuss;
But when she went to pryin' 'round and openin' up
    old sores,
My Betsey rose politely, and showed her out-of-doors!

Since then I don deny but we've had a word or two;
But we've got our ves wide open now, and know just
    what to do:
When one speaks cross the other just meets it with
    a laugh,
And the first one's ready to give up considerable
    more than half.

So make out your bill, Mr. Lawyer: don't stop short
    of an X;
Make it more if you want to, for I have got the
    checks!
I'm richer than a National Bank, with all its treasures
    told:
For I've got a wife at home now that's worth her
    weight in gold.

GONE WITH A HANDSOMER MAN

JOHN

I'VE worked in the field all day, a-ploughin' the "stony
   streak";
I've scolded my team till I'm hoarse; I've tramped
   till my legs are weak;
I've choked a dozen swears (so 's not to tell Jane fibs)
When the plough-p'int struck a stone and the handles
   punched my ribs.

I've put my team in the barn, and rubbed their sweaty
   coats;
I've fed 'em a heap of hay and half a bushel of oats;
And to see the way they eat makes me like eatin' feel,
And Jane won't say to-night that I don't make out a
   meal.

Well said! the door is locked! but here she's left the
   key,
Under the step, in a place known only to her and me;
I wonder who's dyin' or dead, that she's hustled off
   pell-mell:
But here on the table's a note, and probably this will
   tell.

Good God! my wife is gone! my wife is gone astray!
The letter it says, "Good-bye, for I'm a-going away;
I've lived with you six months, John, and so far I've
    been true;
But I'm going away to-day with a handsomer man
    than you."

A han'somer man than me! Why, that ain't much to
    say;
There's han'somer men than me go past here every
    day.
There's han'somer men than me—I ain't of the han'-
    some kind;
But a *lovin'er* man than I was I guess she'll never find!

Curse her! curse her! I say, and give my curses wings!
May the words of love I've spoke be changed to scor-
    pion-stings!
Oh, she filled my heart with joy, she emptied my heart
    of doubt,
And now, with a scratch of a pen, she lets my heart's
    blood out!

Curse her! curse her! say I; she'll some time rue this
    day;
She'll some time learn that hate is a game that two
    can play;
And long before she dies she'll grieve she ever was
    born;
For I'll plough her grave with hate, and seed it down
    to scorn!

As sure as the world goes on, there'll come a time
    when she
Will read the devilish heart of that han'somer man
    than me;
And there'll be a time when he will find, as others do,
That she who is false to one can be the same with two!

And when her face grows pale, and when her eyes
    grow dim,
And when he is tired of her and she is tired of him,
She'll do what she ought to have done, and coolly
    count the cost;
And then she'll see things clear, and know what she
    has lost.

And thoughts that are now asleep will wake up in her
    mind,
And she will mourn and cry for what she has left be-
    hind;
And maybe she'll sometimes long for me — for me —
    but no!
I've blotted her out of my heart, and I will not have
    it so!

And yet in her girlish heart there was somethin' or
    other she had
That fastened a man to her, and wasn't entirely bad;
And she loved me a little, I think, although it didn't
    last;
But I mustn't think of these things — I've buried 'em
    in the past.

I'll take my hard words back, nor make a bad matter
    worse ;
She'll have trouble enough, poor thing ; she shall not
    have my curse ;
But I'll live a life so square — and I well know that I
    can—
That she will always grieve that she went with that
    han'somer man.

Ah, here is her kitchen dress! it makes my poor eyes
    blur ;
It seems, when I look at that, as if 'twas holdin' her.
And here are her week-day shoes, and there is her
    week-day hat,
And yonder's her weddin'-gown : I wonder she didn't
    take that!

'Twas only this mornin' she came and called me her
    " dearest dear,"
And said I was makin' for her a regular paradise here ;
O God! if you want a man to ocnse the pains of hell,
Before you pitch him in just keep him in heaven a
    spell !

Good - bye — I wish that death had severed us two
    apart ;
You've lost a worshipper here—you've crushed a lovin'
    heart.
I'll worship no woman again! but I guess I'll learn to
    pray,
And kneel as *you* used to kneel before you run away.

2

And if I thought I could bring my words on heaven
    to bear,
And if I thought I had some influence up there,
I would pray that I might be, if it only could be so,
As happy and gay as I was a half an hour ago!

JANE (*entering*)

Why, John, what a litter here! you've thrown things
    all around!
Come, what's the matter now? and what 've you lost
    or found?
And here's my father here, a-waiting for supper, too;
I've been a-riding with him — he's that "handsomer
    man than you."

Ha! ha! Pa, take a seat, while I put the kettle on,
And get things ready for tea, and kiss my dear old
    John.
Why, John, you look so strange! Come, what has
    crossed your track?
I was only a-joking, you know; I'm willing to take it
    back.

JOHN (*aside*)

Well, now, if this *ain't* a joke, with rather a bitter
    cream!
It seems as if I'd woke from a mighty ticklish dream;

And I think she "smells a rat," for she smiles at me
    so queer;
I hope she don't; good Lord! I hope that they didn't
    hear!

'Twas one of her practical drives—why *didn't* I under-
    stand!
I'll never break sod again till I get the lay of the
    land.
But one thing's settled with me: to appreciate heaven
    well,
'Tis good for a man to have some fifteen minutes of
    hell!

JOHNNY RICH

RAISE the light a little, Jim,
For it's getting rather dim,
And, with such a storm a-howlin', 'twill not do to
    douse the glim;
Hustle down the curtains, Lu;
Poke the fire a little, Su;
This is somethin' of a flurry, mother, somethin' of a—
    whew!—

Goodness gracious, how it pours!
How it beats ag'in the doors!
You will have a hard one, Jimmy, when you go to do
    the chores!
Do not overfeed the gray;
Give a plenty to the bay;
And be careful with your lantern when you go among
    the hay.

See the horses have a bed
When you've got 'em fairly fed;
Feed the cows that's in the stable, and the sheep
    that's in the shed;

Give the spotted cow some meal,
Where the brindle cannot steal;
For she's greedy as a porker, and as slipp'ry as an eel.

Hang your lantern by the ring,
On a nail, or on a string;
For the Durham calf 'll bunt it, if there's any such a
thing.
He's a handsome one to see,
And a knowin' one is he:
I stooped over t'other morning, and he up and went
for me:

Rover thinks he hears a noise!
Just keep still a minute, boys;
Nellie, hold your tongue a second, and be silent with
your toys.
Stop that barkin', now, you whelp,
Or I'll kick you till you yelp!
Yes, I hear it; 'tis somebody that is callin' out for help.

Get the lantern, Jim and Tom;
Mother, keep the babies calm,
And we'll follow up that halloa, and we'll see where it
is from.
'Tis a hairy sort of night
For a man to face and fight;
And the wind is blowin'— Hang it, Jimmy, bring an-
other light!

*   *   *   *   *   *   *

Ah! 'twas you, then, Johnny Rich,
Yelling out at such a pitch,
For a decent man to help you, while you fell into the
ditch!
'Tisn't quite the thing to say:
But we ought to've let you lay,
While your drunken carcass died a-drinkin' water,
anyway!

And to see you on my floor,
And to hear the way you snore,
Now we've lugged you under shelter, and the danger
all is o'er;
And you lie there, quite resigned,
Whiskey deaf, and whiskey blind,
And it will not hurt your feelin's, so I guess I'll free
my mind.

Do you mind, you thievin' dunce,
How you robbed my orchard once,
Takin' all the biggest apples, leavin' all the littlest
runts?
Do you mind my melon-patch—
How you gobbled the whole batch,
Stacked the vines, and sliced the greenest melons, just
to raise the scratch?

Do you think, you drunken wag,
It was anything to brag,
To be cornered in my hen-roost, with two pullets in
a bag?

You are used to dirty dens;
You have often slept in pens;
I've a mind to take you out there now, and roost you
with the hens!

Do you call to mind with me
How, one night, you and your three
Took my wagon all to pieces for to hang it on a
tree?
How you hung it up, you eels,
Straight and steady, by the wheels?
I've a mind to take you out there now, and hang you
by your heels!

How, the Fourth of last July,
When you got a little high,
You went back of Wilson's counter when you thought
he wasn't nigh?
How he heard some specie chink,
And was on you in a wink,
And you promised if he'd hush it that you never more
would drink?

Do you mind our temperance hall?
How you're always sure to call,
And recount your reformation with the biggest speech
of all?
How you talk, and how you sing,
That the pledge is just the thing—
How you sign it every winter, and then smash it every
spring?

Do you mind how Jennie Green
Was as happy as a queen,
When you walked with her one Sunday, looking sober,
straight, and clean?
How she cried out half her sight,
When you staggered by, next night,
With a shade across your peepers, that you'd picked
up in a fight?

How our hearts with pleasure warmed
When your mother, though it stormed,
Run up here one day to tell us that you truly had re-
formed?
How that very self-same day,
When upon her homeward way,
She ran on you, where you'd hidden, full three-quar-
ters o'er the bay?

Oh, you little whiskey-keg!
Oh, you horrid little egg!
You're a-goin' to destruction with your swiftest foot
and leg!
I've a mind to take you out
Underneath the water-spout,
Just to rinse you up a little, so you'll know what
you're about!

But you've got a handsome eye;
And, although I can't tell why,
Somethin' somewhere in you always lets you get an-
other try:

So, for all that I have said,
I'll not douse you; but, instead,
I will strip you, I will rub you, I will put you into
   bed!

OUT OF THE OLD HOUSE

OUT of the old house, Nancy — moved up into the
    new;
All the hurry and worry is just as good as through!
Only a bounden duty remains for you and I—
And that's to stand on the door-step, here, and bid
    the old house good-bye.

What a shell we've lived in, these nineteen or twenty
    years!
Wonder it hadn't smashed in, and tumbled about our
    ears;
Wonder it's stuck together, and answered till to-day;
But every individual log was put up here to stay.

Things looked rather new, though, when this old
    house was built;
And things that blossomed you, though, would 've
    made some women wilt;
And every other day, then, as sure as day would
    break,
My neighbor Ager come this way, invitin' me to
    " shake."

And you, for want of neighbors, was sometimes blue
    and sad,
For wolves and bears and wild - cats was the nearest
    ones you had ;
But lookin' ahead to the clearin', we worked with all
    our might,
Until we was fairly out of the woods, and things was
    goin' right.

Look up there at our new house !—ain't it a thing to
    see ?
Tall and big and handsome, and new as new can be ;
All in apple-pie order, especially the shelves,
And never a debt to say but what we own it all our-
    selves.

Look at our old log - house — how little it now ap-
    pears !
But it's never gone back on us for nineteen or twenty
    years ;
An' I won't go back on it now, or go to pokin' fun :
There's such a thing as praisin' a thing for the good
    that it has done.

Probably you remember how rich we was that night,
When we was fairly settled, an' had things snug and
    right :
We feel as proud as you please, Nancy, over our house
    that's new,
But we felt as proud under this old roof, and a good
    deal prouder, too.

Never a handsomer house was seen beneath the sun:
Kitchen and parlor and bedroom—we had 'em—all in
    one;
And the fat old wooden clock that we brought when
    we came West,
Was tickin' away in the corner there, and doin' its
    level best.

Trees was all around us, a-whisperin' cheering words;
Loud was the squirrel's chatter, and sweet the songs
    of birds;
And home grew sweeter and brighter — our courage
    began to mount—
And things looked hearty and happy then, and work
    appeared to count.

And here one night it happened, when things was
    goin' bad,
We fell in a deep old quarrel—the first we ever had;
And when you give out and cried, then I, like a fool,
    give in;
And then we agreed to rub all out, and start out life
    ag'in.

Here it was, you remember, we sat when the day was
    done,
And you was a-makin' clothing that wasn't for either
    one;
And often a soft word of love I was soft enough to say,
And the wolves was howlin' in the woods not twenty
    rods away.

Then our first-born baby—a regular little joy—
Though I fretted a little because it wasn't a boy:
Wa'n't she a little flirt, though, with all her pouts and
    smiles?
Why, settlers came to see that show a half a dozen
    miles.

Yonder sat the cradle—a homely, home-made thing,
And many a night I rocked it, providin' you would
    sing;
And many a little stranger brought up with us to
    stay—
And so that cradle, for many a year, was never put
    away.

How they kept a-comin', so cunnin' and fat and small!
How they growed! 'twas a wonder how we found
    room for 'em all;
But though the house was crowded, it empty seemed
    that day
When Jennie lay by the fireplace, there, and moaned
    her life away.

Right in there the preacher, with Bible and hymn-
    book, stood,
" 'Twixt the dead and the living," and "hoped 'twould
    do us good;"
And the little white-wood coffin on the table there was
    set,
And now as I rub my eyes it seems as if I could see
    it yet.

And then that fit of sickness it brought on you, you
    know :
Just by a thread you hung, and you e'en-a'most let go ;
And here is the spot I tumbled, an' give the Lord his
    due,
When the doctor said the fever'd turned, an' he could
    fetch you through.

Yes, a deal has happened to make this old house dear :
Christenin's, funerals, weddin's — what haven't we had
    here ?
Not a log in this buildin' but its memories has got,
And not a nail in this old floor but touches a tender
    spot.

Out of the old house, Nancy — moved up into the
    new ;
All the hurry and worry is just as good as through ;
But I tell you a thing right here, that I ain't ashamed
    to say :
There's precious things in this old house we never can
    take away.

Here the old house will stand, but not as it stood
    before :
Winds will whistle through it, and rains will flood the
    floor ;
And over the hearth, once blazing, the snow-drifts oft
    will pile,
And the old thing will seem to be a-mournin' all the
    while.

Fare you well, old house! you're naught that can feel
    or see,
But you seem like a human being—a dear old friend
    to me;
And we never will have a better home, if *my* opinion
    stands,
Until we commence a-keepin' house in the house not
    made with hands.

OVER THE HILL TO THE POOR-HOUSE

Over the hill to the poor-house I'm trudgin' my
    weary way—
I, a woman of seventy, and only a trifle gray—
I, who am smart an' chipper, for all the years I've told,
As many another woman that's only half as old.

Over the hill to the poor-house—I can't quite make
    it clear!
Over the hill to the poor-house—it seems so horrid
    queer!
Many a step I've taken, a-toilin' to and fro,
But this is a sort of journey I never thought to go.

What is the use of heapin' on me a pauper's shame?
Am I lazy or crazy? am I blind or lame?
True, I am not so supple, nor yet so awful stout;
But charity ain't no favor, if one can live without.

I am ready and willin' an' anxious any day
To work for a decent livin', an' pay my honest way;
For I can earn my victuals, an' more too, I'll be bound,
If anybody is willin' to only have me round.

Once I was young an' han'some — I was, upon my
    soul—
Once my cheeks was roses, my eyes as black as coal;
And I can't remember, in them days, of hearin' people
    say,
For any kind of a reason, that I was in their way!

'Tain't no use of boastin', or talkin' over free,
But many a house an' home was open then to me;
Many a han'some offer I had from likely men,
And nobody ever hinted that I was a burden then!

And when to John I was married, sure he was good
    and smart,
But he and all the neighbors would own I done my
    part;
For life was all before me, an' I was young an' strong,
And I worked my best an' smartest in tryin' to get
    along.

And so we worked together: and life was hard, but
    gay,
With now and then a baby to cheer us on our way;
Till we had half a dozen: an' all growed clean an'
    neat,
An' went to school like others, an' had enough to eat.

An' so we worked for the child'rn, and raised 'em
    every one;
Worked for 'em summer and winter, just as we ought
    to 've done;

3

Only perhaps we humored 'em, which some good folks
    condemn ;
But every couple's own child'rn's a heap the dearest
    to them !

Strange how much we think of our blesséd little
    ones !—
I'd have died for my daughters, I'd have died for my
    sons ;
And God he made that rule of love ; but when we're
    old and gray,
I've noticed it sometimes somehow fails to work the
    other way.

Strange, another thing : when our boys an' girls was
    grown,
And when, exceptin' Charley, they'd left us there
    alone ;
When John he nearer an' nearer came, an' dearer
    seemed to be,
The Lord—of Hosts !—He came one day an' took him
    away from me !

Still I was bound to struggle, an' never to cringe or
    fall—
Still I worked for Charley, for Charley was now my
    all ;
And Charley was pretty good to me, with scarce a
    word or frown,
Till at last he went a-courtin', and brought a wife
    from town.

She was somewhat dressy, an' hadn't a pleasant smile—
She was quite conceity, and carried a heap o' style;
But if ever I tried to be friends, I did with her, I know;
But she was hard and haughty, an' we couldn't make
    it go.

She had an edication, an' that was good for her;
But when she twitted me on mine, 'twas carryin'
    things too fur;
An' I told her once, 'fore company (an' it almost
    made her sick),
That I never swallowed a grammar, or 'et a 'rithmetic.

So 'twas only a few days before the thing was done—
They was a family of themselves, and I another one;
And a very little cottage one family will do,
But I never have seen a mansion that was big enough
    for two.

An' I never could speak to suit her, never could
    please her eye,
An' it made me independent, an' then I didn't try;
But I was terribly humbled, an' felt it like a blow,
When Charley turned ag'in me, an' told me I could go!

I went to live with Susan: but Susan's house was
    small,
And she was always a-hintin' how snug it was for us all;
And what with her husband's sisters, and what with
    child'rn three,
'Twas easy to discover there wasn't room for me.

All of the rest was steady, an' nice, an' good, an' right;
All of the rest was sober—but I was mainly tight;
An' when I "borrowed" two horses, or helped to, just
    for fun—
If I hadn't been drunk as blazes, it never would have
    been done.

But when they sent me to prison, the hardest grief I
    felt
Was when my poor old mother beside me feebly knelt,
And cried and prayed all round me, till I got melted
    down,
And cried as I wouldn't have cried that day for half
    the horses in town.

And with my left arm round her—my right hand lifted
    high—
I swore henceforth to be honest, and sober live and die;
And I went and served my term out, although 'twas
    a bitter pill,
Which many fellows ought to take who probably
    never will.

And when I had served my sentence, I thought
    'twould answer the best
To take the advice of Greeley: "Go West, young man,
    go West!"
And how I came to prosper there, I never could un,
    derstand;
But Fortune seemed to like me—she gave me a win,
    ning hand!

And year after year I prospered, and kept a-going
    ahead ;
And wrote to a trusty neighbor East, to tell 'em that
    I was dead ;
And died a good straight fellow; for I knew it would
    please them more
Than if I had lived to a hundred and twelve — the
    chap that I was before !

But when this trusty neighbor — he wrote a line to
    me—
"Your mother's in the poor - house, a-pining away,"
    says he :
To keep dead any longer — I knew that it wouldn't
    be right ;
So I'd a private resurrection, and started for her that
    night.

And when I came in the old town, my first act was
    to buy
A snug and handsome cottage, which rather seemed
    to my eye
To look just like the old one; I finished it off the
    same ;
You couldn't have told the difference—if you could, *I*
    wasn't to blame !

The same old clock in the corner; the fireplace, wide
    and high,
Sent up the smoke and cinders, and flung them tow-
    ards the sky;

From garret down to cellar — 'twas all the self - same
    thing ;
'Twas good enough for the President — 'twas fine
    enough for a king !

Then over the hill to the poor - house, one blustering
    winter day,
With two fleet nags and a cutter, I swiftly took my way ;
The fleetest nags in the county, and both as black as
    coal—
They very much resembled the pair of horses I stole.

I hitched in front of the poor - house — I opened the
    poor-house door ;
My poor old mother was on her knees, a-scrubbin'
    the kitchen floor !
I coughed a little, on purpose—she started, in surprise—
Rose up, with a scared expression, an' looked me in
    the eyes.

I slowly walked up to her, an' all her troubles' trace
I saw in the lines of sorrow that marred her dear old
    face :
"Mother, O Mother !" I shouted ; "your poor - house
    contract's done ;
An' you henceforth are adopted, by your resurrected
    son !"

She didn't faint nor holloa—but knelt down by my side,
And thanked the Lord for saving her me, till I broke
    down and cried ;

But maybe our ride wasn't merry! and maybe we
    wasn't gay;
And maybe I didn't wrap her up that blustering win-
    ter day!

And maybe, when we had got home, and entered the
    cottage door,
She didn't start back kind of sudden—as if she'd seen
    it before!
And maybe it wasn't pleasant—our cosey evening tea—
With her quite often stoppin', and huggin', and kissin'
    me!

And maybe we didn't live happy, for quite a number
    of years!
And I gained the respect of my neighbors — in spite
    of my brothers' sneers,
And spite of my sisters' caution; who said, as I have
    heard,
That they never could own a brother that had been
    a prison bird!

But I'll bet, when the great bugle rings out its cheer-
    ful notes,
And the good Lord Almighty sorts out His sheep
    and goats,
However my case is settled, if you are there you'll
    see
That my old Christian mother will stand right up
    for me.

UNCLE SAMMY

SOME men were born for great things,
  Some were born for small;
Some—it is not on record
  Why they were born at all;
But Uncle Sammy was certain he had a legitimate
  call.

Some were born with a talent,
  Some with scrip and land;
Some with a spoon of silver,
  And some with a different brand;
But Uncle Sammy came holding an argument in each
  hand.

Arguments sprouted within him,
  And twinkled in his eye;
He seemed to be merely debating
  When average babies cry:
Discussing the question whether 'twas better to live
  or die.

But prejudiced on that question
  He grew from day to day,
And finally he concluded
  'Twas better for him to stay;
And so into life's discussion he argued and argued
  his way.

Through childhood, through youth, into man-
      hood
  Argued and argued he;
And married a simple maiden,
  Though scarcely in love was she;
But he reasoned the matter so clearly she hardly
  could help but agree.

And though at first she was blooming,
  And the new firm started strong,
And though Uncle Sammy loved her,
  And tried to help her along,
She faded away in silence, and 'twas evident some-
  thing was wrong.

Now Uncle Sammy was faithful,
  And various remedies tried;
He gave her the doctor's prescriptions,
  And plenty of logic beside;
But logic and medicine failed him, and so one day
  she died.

He laid her away in the church-yard,
  So haggard and crushed and wan;

Would wink at each other and chuckle,
    And grin at him as he passed,
As to say, "My ambitious old fellow, your whiffletree's
    straightened at last."

Old Uncle Sammy one morning
    Lay down on his comfortless bed,
And Death and he had a discussion,
    And Death came out ahead;
And the fact that SHE failed to start him was only—
    the man was dead.

The neighbors laid out their old neighbor,
    With homely but tenderest art;
And some of the oldest ones faltered,
    And tearfully stood apart;
For the crusty old man had often unguardedly shown
    them his heart.

But on his face an expression
    Of quizzical study lay,
As if he were sounding the angel
    Who travelled with him that day,
And laying the pipes down slyly for an argument on
    the way.

And several younger parties
    Crept round him with quiet feet,
And whispered, "P'rhaps when Uncle Sammy
    Has examined the golden street,
He'll straightway fly to headquarters,
    And argue—concerning his seat."

But God is a God of goodness,
   With love for us all possessed;
And perhaps, now, he took Uncle Sammy,
   And gave him a good night's rest,
And then introduced him to Solomon,
   And said, "Sam, do your best."

TOM WAS GOIN' FOR A POET

The Farmer Discourses of his Son

TOM was goin' for a poet, an' said he'd a poet be;
One of these long-haired fellers a feller hates to see,
One of these chaps forever fixin' things cute and clever;
Makin' the world in gen'ral step 'long to tune an' time;
Cuttin' the earth into slices an' saltin' it down into
    rhyme.

Poets are good for somethin', so long as they stand
    at the head;
But poetry's worth whatever it fetches in butter an'
    bread.
An' many a time I've said it: it don't do a fellow credit,
To starve with a hole in his elbow, an' be considered
    a fool,
So after he's dead the young ones 'll speak his pieces
    in school.

An' Tom he had an opinion that Shakespeare an' all
    the rest,
With all their winter clothin', couldn't make *him* a
    decent vest;

But that didn't ease my labors, or help him among
　　the neighbors,
Who watched him from a distance, an' held his mind
　　in doubt,
An' wondered if Tom wasn't shaky, or knew what he
　　was about.

Tom he went a-sowin', to sow a field of grain;
But half of that 'ere sowin' was altogether in vain.
For he was al'ays a-stoppin', and gems of poetry
　　droppin';
And metaphors, they be pleasant, but much too thin
　　to eat;
And germs of thought be handy, but never grow up
　　to wheat.

Tom he went a-mowin', one broilin' summer's day,
An' spoke quite sweet concernin' the smell of the new-
　　mowed hay.
But all o' his useless chatter didn't go to help the
　　matter,
Or make the grief less searchin' or the pain less hard
　　to feel,
When he made a clip too suddent, an' sliced his
　　brother's heel.

Tom he went a-drivin' the hills an' dales across;
But, scannin' the lines of his poetry, he dropped the
　　lines of his hoss.
The nag ran fleet and fleeter, in quite irregular me-
　　tre;
4

An' when we got Tom's legs set, an' fixed him so's to
  speak,
He muttered that that adventur' would keep him
  a-writin' a week.

Tom he went a-ploughin', and couldn't have done it
  worse ;
He sat down on the handles, an' went to spinnin' verse.
He wrote it nice and pretty—an agricultural ditty ;
But all o' his pesky measures didn't measure an acre
  more,
Nor his p'ints didn't turn a furrow that wasn't turned
  before.

Tom he went a-courtin';—she liked him, I suppose ;
But certain parts of courtin' a feller must do in prose.
He rhymed her each day a letter, but that didn't serve
  to get her :
He waited so long, she married another man from
  spite,
An' sent him word she'd done it, an' not to forget to
  write.

Tom at last got married ; his wife was smart and stout,
An' she shoved up the window and slung his poetry
  out.
An' at each new poem's creation she gave it circula-
  tion ;
An' fast as he would write 'em she seen to their put-
  tin' forth ;
An' sent 'em east an' westward, an' also south an' north.

Till Tom he struck the opinion that poetry didn't pay,
An' turned the guns of his genius, an' fired 'em an-
　　other way.
He settled himself down steady, an' is quite well off
　　already;
An' all of his life is verses, with his wife the first an'
　　best,
An' ten or a dozen child'rn to constitute the rest.

GOIN' HOME TO-DAY

My business on the jury's done — the quibblin' all is
    through—
I've watched the lawyers right and left, and give my
    verdict true;
I stuck so long unto my chair, I thought I would
    grow in;
And if I do not know myself, they'll get me there ag'in.
But now the court's adjourned for good, and I have
    got my pay,
I'm loose at last, and thank the Lord, I'm going home
    to-day.

I've somehow felt uneasy like, since first day I come
    down;
It is an awkward game to play the gentleman in town;
And this 'ere Sunday suit of mine on Sunday rightly
    sets;
But when I wear the stuff a week, it somehow galls
    and frets.
I'd rather wear my homespun rig of pepper - salt and
    gray—
I'll have it on in half a jiff, when I get home to-day.

I have no doubt my wife looked out, as well as any
    one—
As well as any woman could—to see that things was
    done:
For though Melinda, when I'm there, won't set her
    foot out-doors,
She's very careful, when I'm gone, to tend to all the
    chores.
But nothing prospers half so well when I go off to
    stay,
And I will put things into shape, when I get home
    to-day !

The mornin' that I come away, we had a little bout;
I coolly took my hat and left, before the show was out.
For what I said was naught whereat she ought to
    take offence;
And she was always quick at words and ready to com-
    mence.
But then she's first one to give up when she has had
    her say;
And she will meet me with a kiss, when I go home
    to-day.

My little boy—I'll give 'em leave to match him, if
    they can;
It's fun to see him strut about, and try to be a man !
The gamest, cheeriest little chap, you'd ever want to
    see !
And then they laugh, because I think the child re-
    sembles me.

The little rogue! he goes for me, like robbers for
    their prey;
He'll turn my pockets inside out, when I get home
    to-day!

My little girl — I can't contrive how it should happen
    thus—
That God could pick that sweet bouquet, and fling it
    down to us!
My wife, she says that han'some face will some day
    make a stir;
And then I laugh, because she thinks the child re-
    sembles her.
She'll meet me half-way down the hill, and kiss me,
    anyway;
And light my heart up with her smiles, when I go
    home to-day!

If there's a heaven upon the earth, a fellow knows it
    when
He's been away from home a week, and then gets
    back again.
If there's a heaven above the earth, there often, I'll be
    bound,
Some homesick fellow meets his folks, and hugs 'em
    all around.
But let my creed be right or wrong, or be it as it
    may,
My heaven is just ahead of me — I'm going home to-
    day!

OUT O' THE FIRE

YEAR of '71, children, middle of the fall,
On one fearful night, children, we wellnigh lost our
    all.
True, it wa'n't no great sum we had to lose that night,
But when a little's all you've got, it comes to a blessed
    sight.

I was a mighty worker, in them 'ere difficult days,
For work is a good investment, and almost always
    pays;
But when ten years' hard labor went smokin' into the
    air,
I doubted all o' the maxims, an' felt that it wasn't fair.

Up from the East we had travelled, with all of our
    household wares,
Where we had long been workin' a piece of land on
    shares,
But how a fellow's to prosper without the rise of the
    land,
For just two-thirds of nothin'. I never could under-
    stand.

Up from the East we had travelled, me and my folks
  alone,
And quick we went to workin' a piece of land of our
  own;
Small was our backwoods quarters, and things looked
  mighty cheap;
But everything we put in there, we put in there to
  keep.

So, with workin' and savin', we managed to get along;
Managed to make a livin', and feel consid'able strong;
And things went smooth and happy, an' fair as the
  average run,
Till Fate went back upon me square, in the fall of '71.

First thing bothered and worried me, was 'long o' my
  daughter Kate:
Rather a han'some cre'tur', and folks all liked her
  gait.
Not so nice as them sham ones in yeller-covered
  books;
But still there wa'n't much discount on Katherine's
  ways an' looks.

And Katherine's smile was pleasant, and Katherine's
  temper was good,
And how she came to like Tom Smith, I never un-
  derstood;
For she was a mornin'-glory, as fair as you ever see,
And Tom was a shag-bark hickory, as green as green
  could be.

" Like takes to like," is a proverb that's nothin' more
    than trash ;
And many a time I've seen it all pulverized to smash.
For folks in no way sim'lar, I've noticed ag'in and ag'in,
Will often take to each other, and stick together like
    sin.

Next thing bothered and worried me, was 'long of a
    terrible drouth ;
And me an' all o' my neighbors was some'at down in
    the mouth.
And week after week the rain held off, and things all
    pined an' dried,
And we drove the cattle miles to drink, and many of
    'em died.

And day after day went by us, so han'some and so
    bright,
And never a drop of water came near us, day or night;
And what with the neighbors' grumblin', and what
    with my daily loss,
I must own that somehow or other I was gettin'
    mighty cross.

And on one Sunday evenin' I was comin' down the lane
From meetin', where our preacher had stuck and hung
    for rain,
And various slants on things above kept workin' in
    my mind,
And the smoke from Sanders's fallow was makin' me
    almost blind ;

I opened the door kind o' sudden, an' there my Katherine sat,
As cosey as any kitten along with a friendly cat;
An' Tom was dreadful near her—his arm on the back
of her chair—
And lookin' as happy and cheerful as if there was rain
to spare.

"Get out of this house in a minute!" I cried, with all
my might:
"Get out, while I'm a-talkin'!"—Tom's eyes showed a
bit of fight;
But he rose up, stiff and surly, and made me a civil
bow,
And walked along to the doorway, with never a word
of row.

And I snapped up my wife quite surly when she asked
me what I'd said,
And scolded Kate for cryin', and sent her up-stairs to
bed;
And then I laid down, for the purpose of gettin' a
little sleep,
An' the wind outside was a-howlin', and puttin' it in
to keep.

'Twas half-past three next mornin', or maybe 'twas
nearer four—
The neighbors they came a-yellin' and poundin' at my
door;

"Get up! get up!" they shouted: "get up! there's dan-
    ger near!
The woods are all a-burnin'! the wind is blowin' it
    here!"

If ever it happens, children, that you get catched,
    some time,
With fire a-comin' towards you, as fast as fire can
    climb,
You'll get up and get in a hurry, as quick as you can
    budge;
It's a lively season of the year, or else I ain't no
    judge

Out o' the dear old cabin we tumbled fast as we
    could—
Smashed two-thirds of our dishes, and saved some
    four-foot wood;
With smoke a-settlin' round us and gettin' into our
    eyes,
And fire a-roarin' an' cracklin' an' drowndin' all our
    cries.

And just as the roof was smokin', and we hadn't long
    to wait,
I says to my wife, "Now get out, and hustle, you and
    Kate!"
And just as the roof was fallin', my wife she come to
    me,
With a face as white as a corpse's face, and "Where
    is Kate?" says she.

And the neighbors came a-runnin' to me, with faces
    black as the ground,
And shouted, "Where is Katherine? She's nowhere
    to be found!"
An' this is all I remember, till I found myself next
    day,
A-lyin' in Sanders's cabin, a mile an' a half away.

If ever you wake up, children, with somethin' into
    your head,
Concernin' a han'some daughter, that's lyin' still an'
    dead,
All scorched into coal-black cinders—*perhaps* you may
    not weep,
But I rather think it'll happen you'll wish you'd kept
    asleep.

And all I could say, was "Kath'rine, oh Kath'rine,
    come to me!"
And all I could think, was "Kath'rine!" and all that
    I could see,
Was Sanders a-standin' near to me, with pity in his
    eye,
And my wife a-bendin' over me, and tellin' me not to
    cry;

When lo! Tom Smith he entered—his face lit up
    with grins—
And KATE a-hangin' on his arm, as neat as a row of
    pins!

And Tom looked glad, but sheepish; and said, " Excuse me, Squire,
But I 'loped with Kate, and married her an hour before the fire."

Well, children, I was shattered; 'twas more than I could bear—
And I up and went for Kate an' Tom, and hugged 'em then and there!
And since that time, the times have changed, an' life isn't so much bother;
And—Katherine, she's your mother now, and—Thomas Smith's your father!

THE NEW CHURCH ORGAN

They've got a brand-new organ, Sue,
  For all their fuss and search;
They've done just as they said they'd do,
  And fetched it into church.
They're bound the critter shall be seen,
  And on the preacher's right
They've hoisted up their new machine,
  In everybody's sight.
They've got a chorister and choir,
  Ag'in' *my* voice and vote;
For it was never *my* desire
  To praise the Lord by note!

I've been a sister good an' true
  For five-an'-thirty year;
I've done what seemed my part to do,
  An' prayed my duty clear;
I've sung the hymns both slow and quick,
  Just as the preacher read,
And twice, when Deacon Tubbs was sick,
  I took the fork an' led!